FINDING HAPPINESS THROUGH ANGER MANAGEMENT

DREAMLAND PUBLICATIONS
J-128, Kirti Nagar, New Delhi -110 015, India
Tel : +91-11-2510 6050, 2543 5657
E-mail : dreamland@dreamlandpublications.com
Shop online at www.dreamlandpublications.com
Follow us on www.instagram.com/dreamland.publications

Published 2024 by
DREAMLAND PUBLICATIONS
J-128, Kirti Nagar, New Delhi - 110 015, India
Tel : +91-11-2510 6050, 2543 5657
E-mail : dreamland@dreamlandpublications.com
www.dreamlandpublications.com

Printed in India

PREFACE

Anger is an important emotion. People have lots of reasons to be angry. Children get angry, too. For them, anger is like a bitter taste in their mouth. If they don't check and do something that helps it go away, anger can grow and lead to bad consequences.

In the light of the above, 'Anger Management Activity Book' has been designed to help young children explore their feelings and better understand their anger triggers. This book aims to explain and think about what really makes one angry. It will help them develop coping strategies to use and keep their calm.

We are sure that this book will serve as a helping tool to keep children mentally and emotionally healthy.

Contents

WHAT IS ANGER?

Anger is a natural and normal emotion just like joy, sadness, and fear. We all get angry sometimes. Anger is an unpleasant feeling that occurs when we think we have been injured, mistreated, opposed in our long-held views, or when we are faced with obstacles that keep us from attaining personal goals. We get angry if someone says something wrong or mean to us, or if something ruins our plans.

It's normal to feel angry. It is nature's way of telling us that something wrong in our lives has gone anywhere. It happens to everyone – but sometimes anger acts bossy.

DRAW A PICTURE OF WHAT YOU LOOK LIKE WHEN YOU ARE ANGRY?

HOW IT FEELS TO BE ANGRY

How do you know when you are angry? Some children describe their feelings as given below –

I just want to break something!

My hands start to shake!

My eyes become red!

I want the world to get away!

It's like my heart is beating out of control.

Everything inside me jumps as if it has to get out!

It feels like my stomach is tied up in knots!

I feel like shouting and crying.

I feel my head would explode!

I want to take it out on somebody!

DIFFERENT FACES OF ANGER

Angry people can look red in the face or go suddenly very pale. Their eyes look mad, their nostrils may get wider and their lips go thin and tight looking. Often angry people move fast, they may shout, or speak in a loud voice. Sometimes they clench their fists and seem as if they want to hit out at something or someone. They may cry or run away.

EMOTIONS

Draw the faces.

I am happy.

I am sad.

I am sleepy.

I am nervous.

I am angry.

I am hot.

VERBALISING FEELINGS

Sometimes anger can be a way to hide other emotions, like feeling sad, guilty, embarrassed, or disappointed. Because of this, recognising and verbalising the feelings is an important first step to learning to manage our anger over time. Verbalising feelings just means being able to express them out loud, to ourselves, and to others if we need help in solving any problems.

Surprised

Disappointed

Embarrassed

Sad

Worried

Confused

TALK ABOUT YOUR FEELINGS BY DRAWING EXPRESSIONS ON THESE FACES.

UNDERSTANDING THE REASONS FOR ANGER

Though anger is a real and natural emotion, there are reasons to feel angry. It can be caused by both external and internal events. Let's study some reasons for anger. Tick the ones that are talking about something that annoys or angers you.

If someone threatens me.

If no one seems to care about me.

If I want something and can't have it.

If someone treats me unfairly.

If I feel disappointed.

If someone keeps doing something after I've asked them to stop.

If I am not being listened to.

If someone teases me.

If I have to do something that I don't want to do.

If I feel hurt emotionally.

ANGER BEHAVIOURS

When you get angry, you grow frustrated. You yell. You might even become aggressive. Tick the statement you may find yourself thinking or saying when you feel others are doing to make you angry.

If your brother/sister leaves the room looking less clean than perfect.

You are good-for-nothing!

If your friend/classmate gets a better grade than you.

She got an 'A' on that project! Mine was way better. Our teacher is so unfair.

If someone keeps interrupting when you are trying to speak.

If someone accidentally bumps into you.

ANGER MAKES ME

Circle the behaviours that you do when you get frustrated or angry?

- Hit things!
- Kick!
- Hit myself!
- Shut down!
- Slam doors!
- Throw objects!
- Run away!
- Yell and scream!
- Cry!
- Stomp!
- Push or shove!
- Give mean looks!
- Pace back and forth!
- Make gestures!
- Back talk!
- Name-call!
- Clench fists!
- Charge at people!
- Growl!
- Mumble under my breath!
- Huff and puff!

ANGER RULES

It's okay to get mad, but –

DON'T HURT OTHERS!

DON'T HURT YOURSELF!

DON'T DESTROY THINGS!

What are some things you can do instead? Think and write.

ANGER, ANGER!

Anger is a feeling of frustration and dislike when something we perceive as unfair, painful, or bad happens to us.

Anger Frustration Fear Not in Control

Sadness Humiliation Rejection

Guilt Hurt

1. **Anger is a valid emotion.**
   Anger is a completely normal usually healthy, human emotion.

2. **Anger is a secondary emotion.**
   Anger is often the result of another emotion such as sadness or fear.

3. **Anger is caused by internal and external events and affects our thoughts, body, and behaviour.**

4. **Anger behaviour is learned.**
   We learn how to express anger by observing others.

5. **There are healthy ways to express anger — Meditate, Exercise, Breathing**

WHAT MAKES YOU FEEL ANGRY?

All sorts of things can make a person feel angry. Some people get angry when they have to follow a rule they don't like, or when another person is mean to them. List some things that cause you to feel angry.

1 ....

2 ....

3 ....

4 ....

5 ....

6 ....

THINK AND WRITE

Think about the following questions and write —

What are some things that make you angry?

What do you do when you are angry?

Do you feel 'in control' when you are angry?

How do you think you can feel better when you are angry?

PHYSICAL EFFECTS OF ANGER

Each individual is different. Some of the effects of anger might be different for every person. Let's study what you feel when angry.

You may feel hot or cold.

Your heartbeat speeds up.

Your muscles feel tight.

Your breathing might get short and panting.

You could feel shaky, or sick in you tummy.

Your jaw might feel tight.

You may feel almost like crying.

You may feel like screaming or running away.

You may feel like hurting yourself or others.

ANGER SIGNS

Look at the image given below and consider each of the effects of anger.

HOW ANGER FEELS

Describe how different parts of your body feel when you get angry, then write three ways you can calm down your anger.

My eyes feel: ....

My ears feel: ....

My mouth feels: ....

My face feels: ....

My tummy feels ....

My hands feel: ....

My feet feel: ....

WHEN I GET ANGRY, I WILL...

1. ....

2. ....

3. ....

"EXPRESSING ANGER"

I feel ....

(Tell the other person how you feel.)

When ....

(Describe the event that causes your feelings, be specific.)

Please ....

(Tell what you would like to happen in the future.)

IDENTIFYING YOUR TRIGGERS

What makes you upset, irritated, or angry? Sometimes you can't predict situations that will cause you to feel angry, but many times you can identify specific triggers. Identifying your triggers will help you really understand why you are angry. Go through the list below, checking off your triggers. Write 'S' for sometimes, 'A' for always, and 'N' for never.

'S' for sometimes, 'A' for always, 'N' for never.

When your siblings touch your things – ....

When you lose a game or activity – ....

When you don't get help from anyone – ....

When someone doesn't listen to you – ....

When you get a bad grade on a test or project – ....

When you feel someone is trying to control you – ....

When you are being treated unfairly – ....

When you have much work to do – ....

When your friends don't include you – ....

When someone lies to you – ....

When someone calls you a name you don't like – ....

WHAT ARE SOME OTHER ANGER TRIGGERS THAT YOU CAN THINK OF?

I FEEL ANGRY WHEN

ANGER SCALE

There are several different levels of feeling angry, from high to low. Remember, it's not fun feeling mad. Let's check out how your anger scale looks and how you feel on this scale.

Scale	I feel...	I look...
5	I am really mad! I scream. I hurt myself or others. I throw things.	
4	I am angry. I shout. I say things that aren't nice.	
3	Something bothers me. I frown. I don't want to smile.	
2	I am feeling ok. Not great but all is still good.	
1	I feel great! I smile, I laugh and I am relaxed.	

YOUR ANGER SCALE

READ YOUR ANGER SCALE AND CIRCLE THE HIGHEST AND LOWEST FOR TODAY.

0	1	2	3	4	5
calm	bothered	irritated	frustrated	angry	rageful

ANGER THERMOMETER

Do you feel angry a lot of time? What if you had a special thermometer that could read your anger level all day long?

Angry	STOP!
Upset	CALM DOWN RELAX
Sad	THINK ABOUT WHAT YOU REALLY WANT
Happy	THINK ABOUT SOMETHING GOOD
Very Happy	MAKE YOURSELF HAPPY

What are some helpful ways of controlling anger that you can think of?

LEARN TO CONTROL

Sometimes you don't agree with a person. It's okay to have different ideas – but it is not okay to feel angry and hurt anyone with actions or words. You must learn ways to deal with your anger. Here's a list of healthy things you can do when you feel angry. Tick the ones that you might like to try.

Take deep breaths.

Draw your anger.

Do jumping jacks.

Write about your anger.

Count to 100.

Walk away.

Talk to someone.

Play outside.

Listen to music.

Practice a hobby.

BE HONEST

Below are some common reactions to feeling angry. How many of these behaviours have you done? Be honest.

- Roll on the floor!
- Throw things!
- Cry!
- Push!
- Kick!
- Stomp!
- Slam doors!
- Hit yourself!
- Argue!
- Give dirty looks!

ANGER DO'S AND DON'TS

There are some acceptable ways to deal with anger. Let's learn how you can help yourself to deal with anger.

Do's	Don'ts
Calm down before you talk with your friend.	Do not talk when you are really angry.
Pay attention someone is telling you how they feel.	Do not say, "I don't want to hear any of this."
Use 'I' statements, not 'YOU' statements.	Do not blame your friend for all the problems.
Keep a calm tone of voice.	Do not wait until you are so mad that you blow up and start listing ALL of things that are wrong.
Listen really well.	Do not bring up old fights.
Stick to the issue. Talk about the one thing that is bothering you.	Do not use the words 'always' or 'never' for example... "Never talk to me."
Avoid blaming. Focus on fixing the problem.	Do not hit anyone or anything.

WHAT CAN I DO?

Ignore it.
Walk away and let it go.
Go to another activity.
Apologise
SORRY
Tell them to stop!
Wait and cool off.
Talk it out.
Write about it.

CREATE YOUR CALM ZONE

A Calm Zone is a place where you can go when you are starting to feel frustrated or angry. Find a place in your house that you can fill with your toys, games, or activities that can help you calm down so that you can cope with your anger in a healthy way. List the things you can put in your Calm Zone.

YOU CAN CALM YOURSELF DOWN

When you feel angry, unfocused, disappointed, or embarrassed, don't shout, yell, throw things or hurt others. Instead, to help yourself calm down you can do the following activities.

Ask for help

Do yoga or some other simple exercise

Read a book

Draw or colour

Write three positive things you are grateful for

CHECK YOURSELF

It's always better to control anger before it hurts you physically or emotionally. Here are some common signs you can feel when you get angry.

Frowning

Red face

Clenched fists

Easily irritated

Squinty eyes

Emotional, sad, or anxious

If you notice any of these signs, think something is going to be wrong.

EMOTIONAL THERMOMETER

Point to where you think you are on the emotional thermometer.

WAYS TO CALM YOUR ANGER

Here are some quick tips to calm an angry person anywhere.

Breathing – Breathing is one of the best tools for you to control your anger. When you are getting upset, you need to breathe. Let's make breathing fun.

Breathe in for 3.
Hold for 2.
Exhale for 1.
Repeat
Slow it down.

Counting to 100 – Counting is an old-age way everyone uses to do away with anger. All you need to do is focus to count, by doing so; you can send calming signals to the rest of your body. Give it a try. You can try a fun-filled variation. Count backward from 10.

YOU CAN DO THIS

Write some ways in the bubbles to avoid anger.

MAKE A CONNECTION

Write in the red bubbles things that make you feel angry, and write in the blue bubbles your favourite calming ways.

ANGER DO'S

Circle the images that represent healthy anger reactions.

COPING SKILL TOOLS

This is a collection of your coping skill tools that you can use when you are feeling scared, worried, angry, or stressed.

Have a healthy snack.

Dance.

Think good thoughts.

Cuddle or play with your pet.

Walk on your tip toes.

Squeeze a ball.

ANGER MANAGEMENT

Decide what is helpful (do) and what is not helpful (don't) when trying to manage anger. Write the words given below in the right columns.

scream	yell	hit	threaten
kick	ask for help	break the rules	destroy things
remain calm	blame others	relax	find your calm zone

THE DO'S	THE DONT'S
....	....
....	....
....	....
....	....
....	....
....	....
....	....

LET'S PLAY A GAME

Do as directed and check how you can find calm quickly.

YOUR FAVOURITE CALMING TOOL.

WHAT ARE THREE WAYS OF HANDLING YOUR ANGER?

WHAT MAKES YOU SMILE?

DRAW YOUR FACE WHEN YOU ARE ANGRY.

SHARE HOW YOU BEHAVE WHEN YOU ARE ANGRY.

DESCRIBE IN ONE WORD HOW YOU FEEL IN ANGER.

CALM DOWN

What can you do to calm down at each temperature?

RED ZONE Angry/Aggressive- Out of Control	Breathe three times Stomp your feet
ORANGE ZONE Agitated - Fearful of Losing Control	Change what you are doing Shout loudly
YELLOW ZONE Sad or Anxious or Nervous	Think of something happy Kick things
BLUEZONE Silly or Unsure	Tear your book keep up good things
LIGHT BLUE ZONE Calm and Happy	Cry Dance and sing

FEELINGS CHECK-UP

Do a feelings check-up by circling the words given in each card that best describe your position.

SAD

Worried
Guilty
Tired
Lonely
Scared
Bored
Unhappy
Depressed

ANGRY

Agitated
Jealous
Mad
Confused
Annoyed
Frustrated
Fed up
Anxious

CALM

Kind
Loving
Relaxed
Peaceful
Grateful
Thankful
Quiet
Still

HAPPY

Joyful
Bright
Positive
Brave
Surprised
Cheery
Excited
Content

MY ANGER BUTTONS

Fill in each button with something that makes you angry. These are the things or situations that "push your buttons."

FINAL TEST

When I'm Angry

What I think....

What I say....

What I feel inside...

What I do....

What my body feels